WordPress for Beginners: A Step by Step Guide - Build a Site within Minutes.

Ready your Search-Engine-Optimized Website in FIVE, simple, steps!

Description

All it takes to create a website using WordPress are five simple steps, at the end of which you will have a search-engine-optimized, responsive, and visitor friendly website.

This guide divides the whole process of creating a website into five, easy to follow steps. It starts with laying out the basic terminologies, followed by registering your domain name and selecting a hosting service. Next, you will be installing the necessary items, creating content, configuring your website, and finally market your web-content!

With this guide, anyone can make great websites. You need no experience in coding or professional web development—all you will be required to do is read, type, and click!

Contents

  Installing WordPress.. 23

    Quick Install: Hostgator's 1-Click WordPress Install Feature 24

  Installing Themes... 27

    What is a Responsive Web Theme? 29

    Some Responsive Web Themes 29

  Important Plugins to Install 37

    Plugins to Optimize Your Website for Search Engines 37

    Plugins to Optimize Your Website for Visitors................................. 42

    Plugins to Optimize Your Social Media Marketing........................... 46

    Found More Plugins That You Like? 48

  Installing Plugins... 49

    Manually Installing the Plugins 52

Step#4: Upload Some Content.. 55

  The Types of Content 55

    Pages... 55

    Posts 56

  Deleting Default Content... 56

  Adding New Content.. 58

    Adding Posts.. 58

    Adding Pages... 61

Introduction

On the inside, WordPress is an extremely complex piece of software that makes creating websites *on it* a very simple process. This ease of use is the result of its diverse range of options that allow the website developer great room of control and creativity. WordPress and its accompanying ecosystem of website themes and plugins allow you to customize the designs and the functionality of your website without writing a single line of code yourself.

Yet, this diversity of options is also a bane for people who are creating a website using WordPress for the first time. The range of options can become overwhelming. As a result, people who are new to creating websites using WordPress feel at a loss as to where their journey should start.

This guide is intended to rectify this problem. This is done by dividing the whole process of creating great websites on WordPress into simpler steps. We have broken the process into 5 consecutive modules which any new-comer can easily follow as well as keep track of.

Overview of the Guide

Chapter One

It is necessary to know about the important elements that make a website. It gives you an idea of the areas you will need to work on. As a result, you'll be able to have a glimpse at the bigger picture.

Hence, the first chapter "School Yourself" will familiarize you with the basics of creating a website. It will state and elaborate the four basic components of a website.

This is followed by an in-depth introduction to WordPress, the platform of your choice.

Chapter Two

Creating a website is like creating a new being on the internet. Hence, you have to have a name for it, register that name, and find a place for it to reside in. For a website it's name is referred to as a registered domain name, whereas you have to find a hosting service to provide a place for your website.

This chapter is intended to guide you through the process of registering a domain name and hosting it on a server. Hence, at the end of this chapter you will have become the owner of web-space registered to your name.

Chapter Three

A hosted website is still dysfunctional as long as it does not have a proper platform to build itself on. Furthermore, it needs a theme and plugins to increase its functionality as well as décor.

This chapter guides you through the process of installing the WordPress platform, themes, and plugins.

The chapter elaborates Hostgator's handy feature through which WordPress can be installed with a single click. Furthermore, you will also be introduced to the concept of responsive website designs (websites that can easily be viewed on any type of mobile screen without compromising the user experience).

Finally, a list of important themes and plugins are introduced. They will definitely make your website standout in search results and increase the user-experience of all the visitors that come to your website.

By the end of this chapter you will have a functional website ready to display all the content you want to upload.

Chapter Four

This chapter will guide you through the process of creating and uploading content to your website. The chapter beings by differentiating between the types of content you will be interacting with, followed by creating pages and uploading posts.

By the end of this chapter your website will have 4 primary web pages (Home, Contact, Blog, and About) that have been configured and optimized individually to serve their intended purposes.

Chapter Five

It's time to tune all the elements of your website so that they can work in together in harmony. Hence, this chapter is dedicated to configuring your website's theme, content and plugins.

You will be introduced to the wide range of settings available in the WordPress' dashboard. Hence, by the end of this chapter you will be able to easily tweak the settings either of the website as a whole as well as the pages individually.

Well then, let us get started with those basics!

Step #1: School Yourself – The Basics of Website Building

What Websites Are Made Of

Making a website may seem a daunting task but if you gain a firm grasp of its basics then you will find it much easier. What's more, you will enjoy building it!

A functional website is comprised of four primary components:

1. Domain name

2. Hosting service

3. Platform

4. Theme

Understanding each of these terms and concepts will give you a firm grasp of how a website functions and will boost your confidence in making one. We'll discuss each of these terms separately.

Domain Name

This is the name of your website. A domain name also acts as an easy to remember address to your website. It tells people where to find you on the internet.

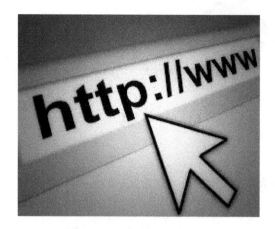

If you were to think of your website as building a home or an office then a domain name is its digital address. Take the example of a website such as **www.your-worpress-site.com**. This is the address that people will search for when they want to visit your "web-place".

Hosting Service

Your website needs a place from which it can function 24/7. This is where a website hosting service comes in. A website hosting service such as Hostgator is a company that provides your website a home on the internet. This home is called a computer server where your website will reside. The server is just a special computer with special software to transmit and display your website across the globe.

In other words, a hosting service provides you the "land" to build your home/office on. Just like a store needs land for the building as well as all the equipment, your website will require a place where all your uploaded files and images can be stored.

A Platform

This is the software that will give you the tools for constructing a website on your web server. Consider this as the foundation - the supporting structure of your website. Just like a house cannot be built without a proper foundation that can support the whole house, a website cannot be built without a platform. Hence, it is the software you will be interacting with most extensively.

The good news is that you don't have to build this platform. WordPress is the pre-built platform that can easily be installed on your web host's server. It also includes many features that will increase your interactivity with customers.

WordPress in Detail

WordPress is an open-source website platform. It has been in service since 2003 and now powers and supports millions of websites and blogs. This includes companies large and small – even Fortune 500 companies such as GM, Sony, UPS, Sony, eBay, and Best Buy are known to have used WordPress to host their content! The cause of its popularity is its ease of use. It is one of the most user-friendly, self-hosted platforms out there. Furthermore, not only does it have an enormous base of plugins that add greater functionality to your site, WordPress is very stable, secure, and able to power any kind of website you intend to build.

WordPress Basics

The WordPress platform can be divided into four different components. These include:

1. WordPress CMS

2. Themes

3. Plugins

4. Widgets

We'll briefly discuss the role of each component in building your website briefly.

WordPress CMS

CMS stands for "Content Management System". Interestingly, WordPress itself is built around the concept of a content management system. In other words, the platform is designed to easily manage all of the content on your website.

As a result, you do not require any coding experience nor do you have to learn or master any coding language. WordPress CMS has done all that for you. Whenever you will be adding or editing content, adding new themes and plugins, WordPress will be converting your clicks into proper coding in the background. Hence, you and your customers and readers will have a great interactive interface while the search engines will find the website that meets their SEO (Search Engine Optimization) criteria.

Themes

WordPress requires that you select a theme setting up your website. You can either select from the themes pre-installed with WordPress or search the internet – you will find both free and paid themes to meet your needs.

Themes affect the layout and design of your site. They also add more functionality to the design. WordPress lets you easily change the basics of a theme — for example, you can change the color of your website, or change the location of your sidebar from the left to the right by simply clicking the options.

Though WordPress allows most themes to be customized using built-in options, some themes may use their own framework. Such themes let you drag-and-drop customizations. Most themes, however, provide simple point-and-click operations for making configuration changes.

Plugins

Plugins are additional software either by WordPress or third party companies that add greater functionality to your WordPress website. Examples include adding a contact form and gallery etc. Think of anything and chances are that someone has developed a plugin for that functionality. There are literally thousands of different plugins available free of cost, and the best thing is they are almost always free, simple to install, and easy to configure.

Widgets

WordPress also lets you add more *features* to your website. Using widgets you can further increase the interactivity visitors can enjoy when surfing through your website. A widget is normally added to the side bars. Common examples include adding a search widget so that people can search through your website, or a navigation bar, etc.

The best part about widgets is that not only do they add more features to your website, adding them is very simple — all you have to do is find the right widget and drag-and-drop them in the highlighted widget area.

End Remarks

If all the talk about WordPress intimidated you even a little, then we want to reassure you that WordPress is very easy to use.

WordPress was developed so that non-technical people could eventually have a user-friendly interface for managing their website. When the recent release of WordPress's latest version was released some 65 million people downloaded!

Ease of use is the exact reason why WordPress was developed in the first place. And that is another reason why WordPress has become the most popular blogging platform in the world.

A Theme

This is a set of files and images with which you will adorn your website. A theme allows you to change the look and functionality of your website. Installing a theme in WordPress requires a few mouse clicks. After you have installed a theme you can get more creative and make different adjustments to increase its functionality as well as the way it looks.

Selecting a theme is like selecting the paint for your home/office. It adds a more humane and colorful look to your website. A vast number of themes are available in WordPress. You can also download more files from the internet.

Hopefully, you understand the basic components of a website that you will be working on.

Step #2: Name and Host Your Website

Now it's time to brainstorm a name for you website, register that domain name, and get it hosted. We'll begin by selecting and registering a domain name.

Selecting a Domain Name

First think of a name for your website. Remember that a domain name can be as long as 67 characters AND that you won't always find your choice on the internet. Furthermore, you can only use letters, number, and dashes in your domain name.

A rule of thumb while brainstorming is that your website's name should:

1. Specify the niche your work/business

2. Give some hint about the webpage

3. Be easy to read and remember

The following are a few tips that you might help you come up with a better domain name:

Use Only These Suffixes: .com, .net, or .org for your domain.

These suffixes give the domain name a professional touch. Furthermore, people associate authority with such suffixes and hope to find relevant content on these sites.

Avoid Hyphens and Numbers

Try to find and register longer domains without adding numbers and hyphen breaks. Hyphens and numbers make it harder to remember the name. It also looks cheaper than a domain that only has letters.

Keep it Short

Make your brand easier to remember and your site easier to find. Longer names mean that a lot of people might end up on another website because they missed a hyphen or a helping verb.

Make it Unique

Make it catchy and memorable. You don't want your visitors and customers confusing your website for another established one. While registering you will know whether the same name has been registered with another suffix like www.your-worpress-site.com may already be registered as **www.your-worpress-site.net.**

Advertise with Your Domain Name

Use a domain name that matches what's on your website. It can gather you a lot of traffic. If a visitor surfing the net looks at your domain name he/she should have a general idea what your website is about. If your website is about trekking and the domain name is about resorts, it will definitely put off the visitor.

With this you are ready to start on the path to selecting a domain that you can live with for years to come. Take your time, because after you register the domain, the only way to change it is to purchase another one.

Registering a Domain Name – Signing Up For Web Hosting

There are many web hosting services available on the internet such as Hostgator, Bluehost, and DreamHost etc. Each offers its own set of packages. We will be guiding you to hosting a website using Hostgator.

1. To get started, visit the Hostgator home page and click "View Web Hosting Plans" button in the middle of the page.

This will lead you to a second page where you will be asked to select the hosting plan you want. The plans are divided according to Package Type and Billing Cycle. Hence, your first task will be to select the plan you need followed by the billing cycle from the drop down menu.

We advise using the "Hatchling" plan for beginners. This plan allows you to register only one domain under your account, whereas the "Baby" plan will let you put unlimited domains under your account but at a greater cost. Start with the "Hatchling" plan and once you have a firm grip of the website building process you can upgrade to the "baby" plan.

Furthermore, keep in mind that the billing cycles range from one month to three years. The longer you pay for upfront, the less you will have to pay every month.

2. Once you have selected the plan click "Order Now" to continue to the next page to enter your billing information.

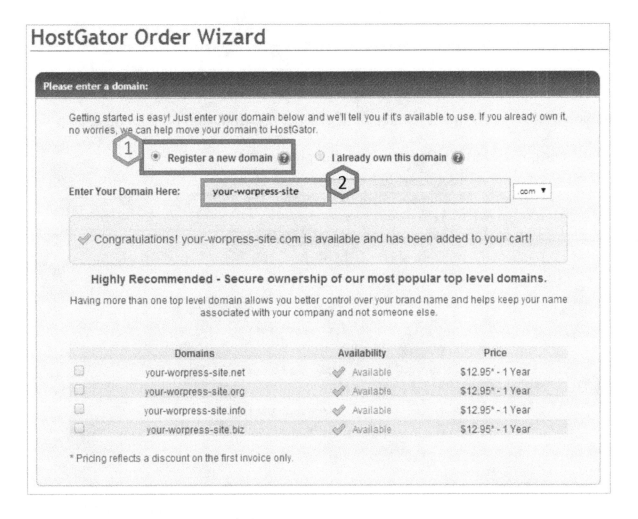

You will be prompted to select whether you want to register a new domain, or if you have a domain name you'd like to transfer to Hostgator. In case this is your first domain, enter the new domain you want to register, or if you already have a registered domain name add that.

Hostgator will then ask you to either confirm or change the Package Type you want followed by the billing Cycle.

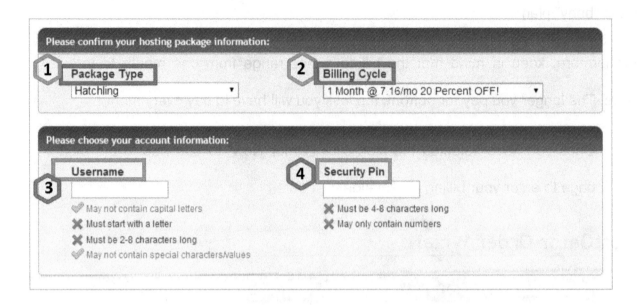

Select your choice of payment (Credit Card or PayPal). Enter the appropriate billing information or go through the PayPal check out process.

Please enter your billing information:

Billing Information		Payment Information
Email		● Credit Card
First Name		○ PayPal
Last Name		
Company		Name on Card
Home Phone		
Cell Phone		Credit Card Number
Address		
Address 2		Expiration Date
City		
State	Alabama	CVV Code
Zip Code		
Country	United States	Help: Where is my CVV Code?

Hostgator facilitates you with additional add-ons (plugins if you may). If you already have some experience with building a website on another platform, then select the ones you think are needed, otherwise scroll down to skip this screen.

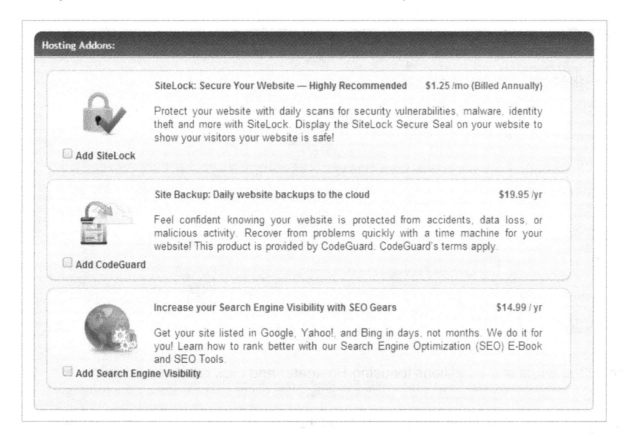

In case you have any coupons available for the hosting service validate it by adding it in the coupon code dialog box.

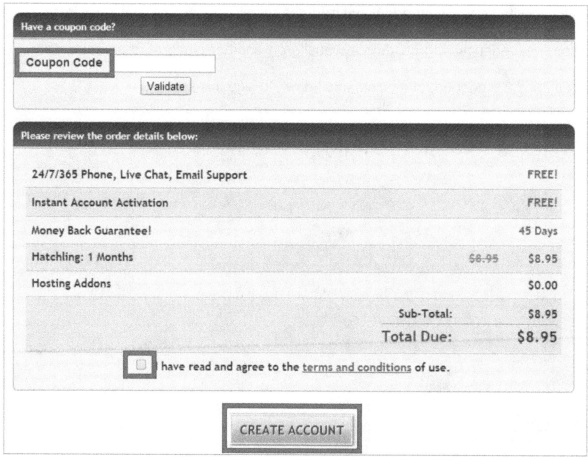

Accept the terms and conditions for using Hostgator and click create an account.

Congratulations! You have finally completed registering and hosting your domain with Hostgator.

Hostgator will send you a "Welcome" email containing all of the information you need for logging in to and managing your server.

Step #3: Install – WordPress, Theme, and Plugins

[One Click Install Feature]

Installing WordPress

One of the best features of using Hostgator is that it lets you install WordPress on your hosted website with a few mouse-clicks. This is especially relieving for new website builders as it takes off the anxiety of manually setting-up WordPress on your hosted website.

By the time you have followed through to this chapter you would already have a Hostgator account and be able to easily login to its dashboard through the c-panel.

From then onwards it's a simply journey of a few scrolls and mouse clicks to get WordPress automatically downloaded *and* installed on your website.

Quick Install: Hostgator's 1-Click WordPress Install Feature

1. Login to Hostgator through the c-panel (Your domain name/c-panel):

<u>www.your-worpress-site.com/cpanel</u>

2. Once on the dashboard, scroll down and locate software/services on the right hand side.

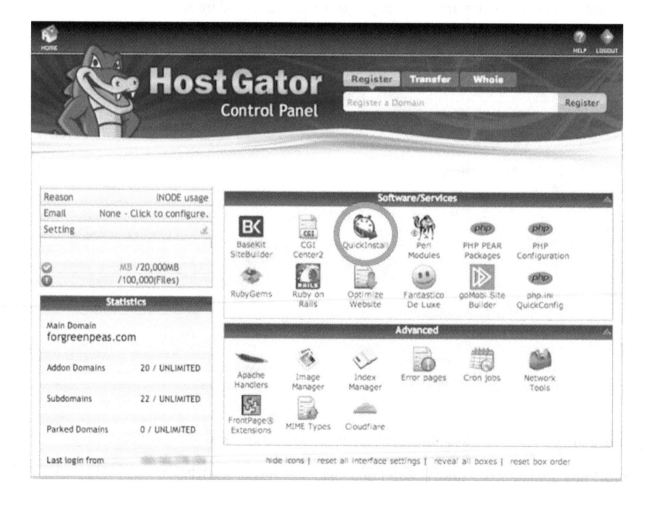

3. Click on the **Quick Install** icon

4. From the side bar on your left locate **Blog Software**

5. Click WordPress then Click Continue

6. An application URL form will appear. Here you have the option of installing WordPress in a folder on your domain or to make WordPress as your main domain.

   E.g. if you want to install WordPress in a folder named "blog" on your website then write —www.your-worpress-site.com/blog

7. Add the correct admin email where Hostgator will email you the password;

8. Click **Install Now;**

Enable Auto Upgrades:	☑
Admin Email:	
Blog Title:	
Admin Username:	
First Name:	
Last Name:	

📄 **Install Now!**

9. Hostgator's Quick Install will immediately download WordPress.

10. Check your email. Hostgator would have sent you the Username and Password for your Admin area of your website.

11. Once you have received the email, use the password to login to WordPress admin area

It is advisable to reset password by clicking **Users**> **Your Profile**> scroll down enter the new password and click **Update Profile**.

Installing Themes

To install a theme on WordPress:

1. Download the theme— save it somewhere convenient. Unzip it;

2. Log on to your WordPress dashboard at:

www.your-worpress-site.com/wp-admin

3. Go to, **"Appearance"** > **"Themes"**;

4. Click on the, **"Upload"** link;

5. Select **"Choose File"** and navigate to the location where you had downloaded the theme;

6. Select the theme then click "**Open**";

7. Install the theme by clicking "**Install Now**";

8. Once the theme has successfully installed:

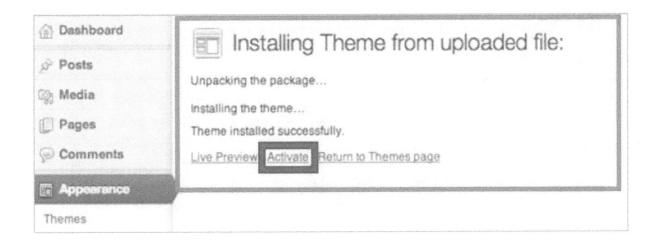

9. Click, "**Activate**.

You can find a diverse range of free themes suited for your website, but not all of them will make your website easily viewable on mobile devices such as smart phones, tablets, PCs, etc. Make your website easily accessible from mobile devices using responsive themes.

What is a Responsive Web Theme?

A theme that can easily cater different screen sizes by **(1)** automatically sensing the screen size and **(2)** realigning and resizing itself for that screen, is known as a responsive web theme. Hence, a visitor visiting a website with a responsive theme will not have to find the sidebars or the navigation-pane by sliding and swiping their screens. The theme will resize and realign itself to display the content and everything else on their screen.

Some Responsive Web Themes

A diverse range of free responsive themes for WordPress are available on the internet. Some of them include the following:

1. Responsive

http://wordpress.org/themes/responsive

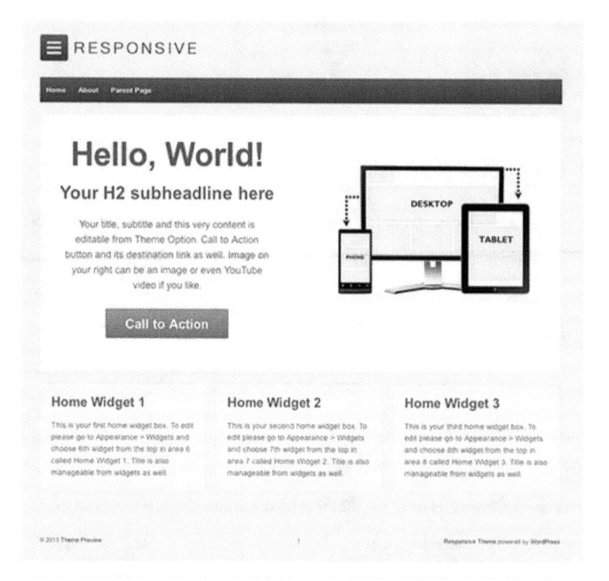

2. Simple Grid

http://www.dessign.net/simple-grid-theme-responsive/

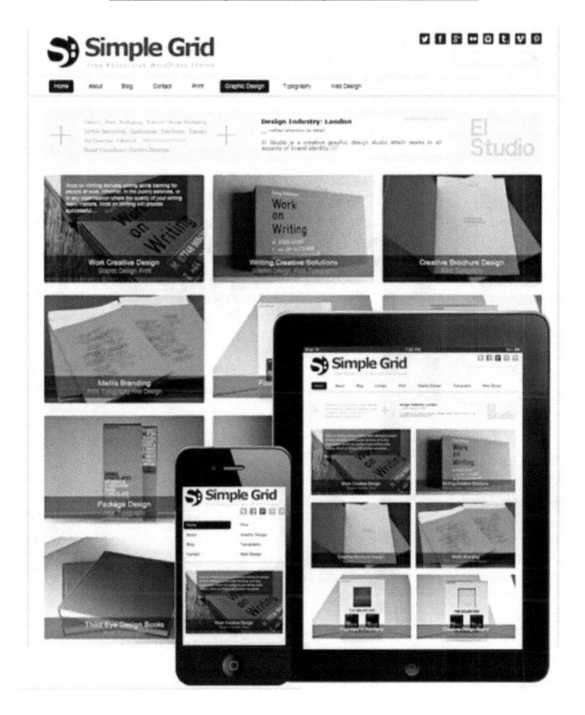

3. Gridly

http://www.eleventhemes.com/gridly-theme/

4. Daily Post Pro

http://wplook.com/dailypost

5. Design Folio

http://www.presscoders.com/designfolio/

6. Whiteboard

http://whiteboardframework.com/

7. Tumble Press

http://colorlabsproject.com/themes/tumblepress/

8. Ari

http://www.elmastudio.de/en/themes/ari/

9. Caroline

http://themeforest.net/item/coraline-ajax-and-responsive-wordpress-theme/2502929

Important Plugins to Install

Plugins to Optimize Your Website for Search Engines

To make your website stand out on every search engine's radars—and hence increase its ranking on the search engine results page— install the following plugins.

WordPress SEO by Yoast

http://wordpress.org/plugins/wordpress-seo/

Search Engine Optimization (SEO) is an integral factor in determine how often your website will rank high in search engine results page. With WordPress SEO, you donot have to worry about being an SEO expert to make your website worthy of notice by search engines. This fantastic plugin by Yoast will greatly aid you with on-page SEO.

This plugin lets you easily align your website with the SEO demands of Google like well-organized permalinks, proper redirection of your website's pages, setting up Google Authorship, etc. The plugin not only reminds you of SEO factors that need your attentions (Sitemaps, Meta Links) but also optimizes them automatically.

Furthermore, this plugin offers you an easy to understand and use "SEO Checklist" to be used while creating content for your website (blog posts, web content, etc). The plugin displays the checklist as a series of Red, Yellow, and Green dots for technical aspects of content SEO. The greener your checklist, the better will be your posts.

Google XML Sitemaps

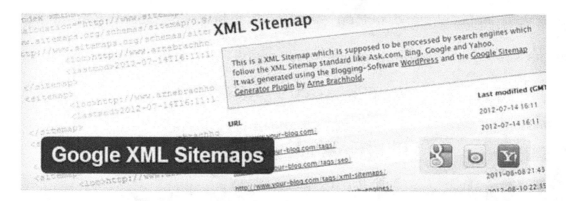

http://wordpress.org/plugins/google-sitemap-generator/

As soon as your website blips in a search engine's radar—web crawlers (aka Spiders) will come your way. These crawlers analyze how friendly is your website's design (for the search engine as well as visitors). The best SEO practice in this regard is to give the search engine a map of your website —known as a sitemap. Once you have a proper sitemap, the search engine will automatically favorably list your website (known as indexing).

The Google XML Sitemaps plugin automates the whole process of creating a sitemap. Furthermore, it regularly updates the sitemaps and can be set to automatically notify search engines of the latest updates. As a result your latest posts get seen a lot quicker.

W3 Total Cache

http://wordpress.org/plugins/w3-total-cache/

How fast a website loads on a computer is of great concern to search engines. When someone searches online, the search engines (Google, Bing, Yahoo, and others) have to go through billions of indexed web pages to match and show the best results for that single query. Their major concern is to display websites that are likely to give the best user experience to the visitor. If your website is a slow poke (meaning it uses extra memory) then the search engine will rank it poorly.

The W3 Total Cache will dramatically increase your website's speed by optimizing several memory consuming areas, the most important being:

1. Browser caching

2. Page cache

3. Object cache

4. Database cache, and more

As a result, not only will your website get ranked better by search engines, it will also add to the user experience of all the visitors.

SEO Friendly Images

http://wordpress.org/plugins/seo-image/

Google Images is another natural portal that can greatly increase healthy traffic to your website. This is only possible if the images you have posted on your website are optimized to get easily found by the portal.

SEO Friendly Images automatically adds the ALT and TITLE attribute to images. This will significantly increased your visibility in Google Images and hence can boost the entire webpage's SEO.

SEO Ultimate

http://wordpress.org/plugins/seo-ultimate/

The *True* All-in-One WordPress SEO Plugin.

Title Tags. Open Graph. Auto Linking. Twitter Cards. Siloing. Meta Descriptions. Affiliate Link Masking. Author Images. 404 Tracking. Canonical Tags. Google Rich Snippets. Noindex. And more.

20+ modules. Hundreds of features. For free.
Install your copy today.

This another intuitive SEO mega plugin that can tunnel your website for any SEO irrelevant element. The Deeplink Juggernaut is one of its major feature through which it searches the content on your site for the keyword phrases that you have specified and **automatically** links them to a URL! If you were to use this feature judiciously you can easily prevent spam and increase traffic. Other great features that you can ontrol include:

1. Plugin Settings Manager

2. SEO Ultimate Widgets

3. Meta Robot Tags Editor

4. Permalink Tweaker

5. Title Tag Rewriter

6. Meta Description Editor

Plugins to Optimize Your Website for Visitors

To give your visitors a great user-experience, install the following plugins.

WP Smush.it

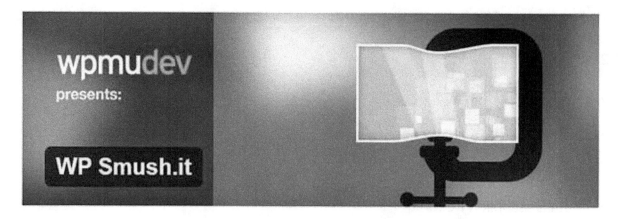

http://wordpress.org/plugins/wp-smushit/

Images can enhance the impact of your content as well as negatively affect the user experience. Heavy images take greater time to download and as your website begins to attract more visitors, it becomes harder for the server to effectively display them to all the visitors.

The WP Smush.it plugin (developed by Yahoo) significantly reduces the file size of your images by removing all the information that will not affect the quality of user experience.

BJ Lazy Load

http://wordpress.org/plugins/bj-lazy-load/

This plugin will help reduce the loading time of image intensive pages by discretely loading images instead of loading all the images on a single webpage at once.

Normally, when you open a webpage, all the images on that page get downloaded in bulk. This greatly strains the resources of your server as well as the visitor's computer. As a result, it takes more time for your website to load.

BJ Lazy Load simply loads up the images that are immediately visible to the visitor—hence images lower down the page get loaded only when the visitor scrolls down toward them.

Akismet

http://wordpress.org/plugins/akismet/

Adding a comments section on your website allows you to engage with your readers on a more personal level. It can also become a hotspot for spammers hoping to redirect traffic to other (suspect) websites. If left unchecked and uncontrolled, it reflects negatively with search engines.

Akismet is an easy to configure spam blocker that will help you get rid of these spammy comments —*automatically*. Every time a visitor leaves a comment, it is first directed through the Akismet service to see whether it is a spam or not.

Disqus Comment

http://wordpress.org/plugins/disqus-comment-system/

Make your comment section appear more unique by using a more professional looking comments section instead of the default WordPress comment section. Disqus will make commenting on your site easier as well as more engaging.

Additionally, Disqus is compatible with Akismet and allows you to know who has commented/replied to your post. It has a ton of great features that will significantly increase the control you have over moderating comments. Some of the important features include:

1. Threaded comments and replies

2. Notifications and reply by email

3. Subscribe and RSS options

4. Aggregated comments and social mentions

5. Powerful moderation and admin tools

6. Full spam filtering, black-lists and white-lists, and more!

Search engines recognize websites that have built a good following not only on the social media but also by engaging visitors on a personal level (comments). Fully utilize the power of user reviews by installing Akismet and Disqus.

404 Redirected

http://wordpress.org/plugins/404-redirected/

Broken links present a serious problem for your website as they cause you to lose a lot of traffic. The other problem with broken links is that you cannot know if your webpage has a broken link unless you check it yourself, and you cannot possibly check all your pages regularly enough.

Additionally, if these are left unmonitored and unresolved long enough, search engines like Google will stop ranking thee pages. As a result your website will lose it status in the search results.

The 404 Redirected plugin shows all the URLs on your website that are returning 404 errors. It resolves this by automatically creating a 301 redirect because of which the visitor is directed to the pages on your site that are fully functional.

Plugins to Optimize Your Social Media Marketing

Expand your fan-base, boost your following and reposts, and redirect more traffic to your web pages by making it easier for visitors to follow you on social media platforms. Install the following plugins!

WordPress Popular Posts

http://wordpress.org/plugins/wordpress-popular-posts/

WordPress Popular Posts allows you to advertise your most popular posts and other content (audio, video, images, etc)—and hence direct more traffic towards them.

With this plugin installed you can easily list blogs that have been most popular within a specific time range (last month, last week, past 24 hrs, etc). Additionally you can check the stats on your most popular posts—find out list posts by number of comments, day to day views, or average views per day.

Furthermore, the plugin lets you design your own layout for displaying popular posts on your theme. Use WP-Post Ratings support to show visitors how readers have rated them!

Floating Social Bar

Floating Social Bar *Increases social media shares

http://wordpress.org/plugins/floating-social-bar/

Make it easier for your visitors to share your posts. This can significantly increase the traffic to your website.

This plugin *fixes* all the share-buttons on top of your page. Hence even when the visitor scrolls down the page, the sharing bar is always viewable. The best part about this plugin is that it has been designed to work well on mobile devices as well.

Easy Social Icon

http://wordpress.org/plugins/easy-social-icons/

Let your visitors know where to find you on social media by adding uniquely designed social media icons. Visitors can easily navigate to your social media pages and subscribe to receive future updates.

This plugin not only lets you display icons to your social sites but also lets you design and customize the look of each icon. Hence you can match the icons according to the theme you have selected for your website.

Found More Plugins That You Like?

In case you have come across some other plugin that you just want to install to your website, then it will be wise to keep track of their impact on your website's performance. Do this by installing:

Plugin Performance Profiler

http://wordpress.org/plugins/p3-profiler/

With this plugin installed you can easily locate plugins that are slowing down your website.

Installing Plugins

Log in to your WordPress dashboard through:

www.your-worpress-site.com/wp-admin

1. Go to "**Plugins**" and "**Add New**" from the left-hand side;

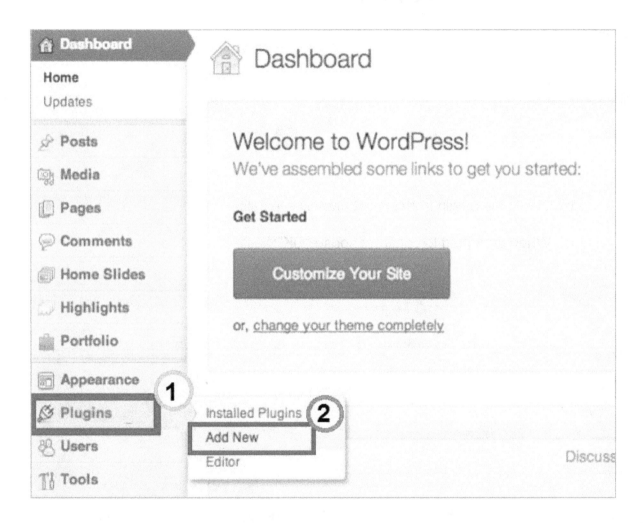

2. You have the option of searching for a plugin:

    a. To search, simply click the "Search" field, and type the name of the plugin and then click "Search Plugins" and wait for the results to be displayed;

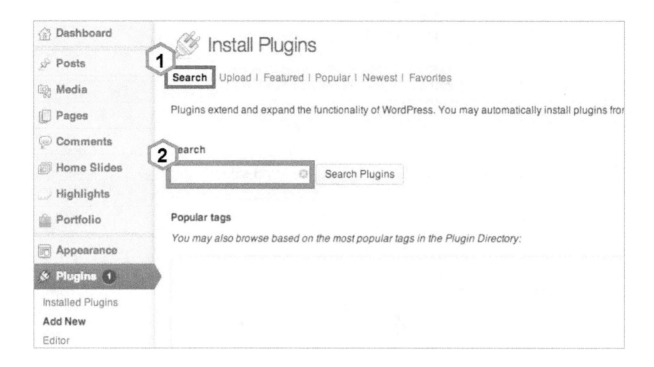

b. Select the plugin from the list and click install;

c. When prompted to confirm choose "OK";

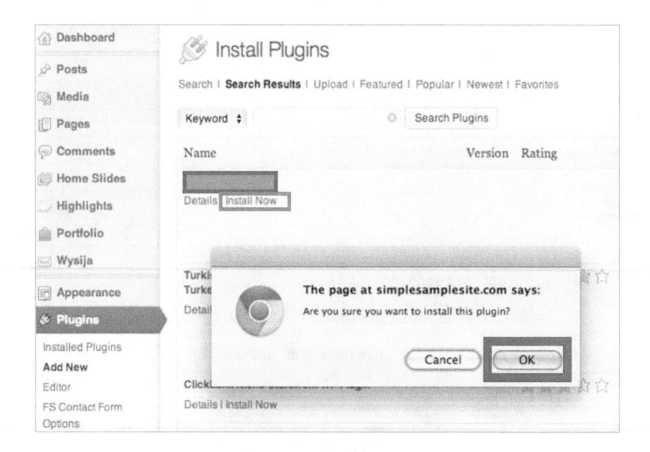

d. The plugin will install automatically, and will give you a series of messages letting you know what is going on;

e. After it finishes, you will see an, "**Activate Plugin**" link appear;

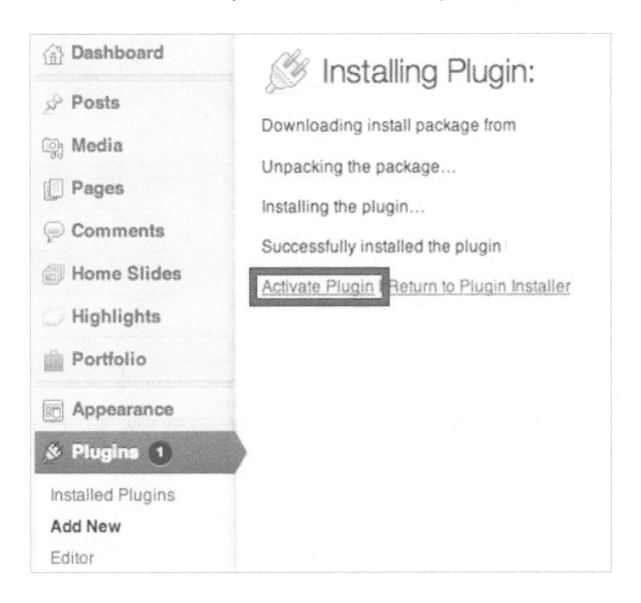

f. Click on that link to finish the installation.

g. You'll then be taken to the Plugin page where you'll have a list of the plugins installed on your website

h. Finally, click the, "**Install Plugins**" button down below.

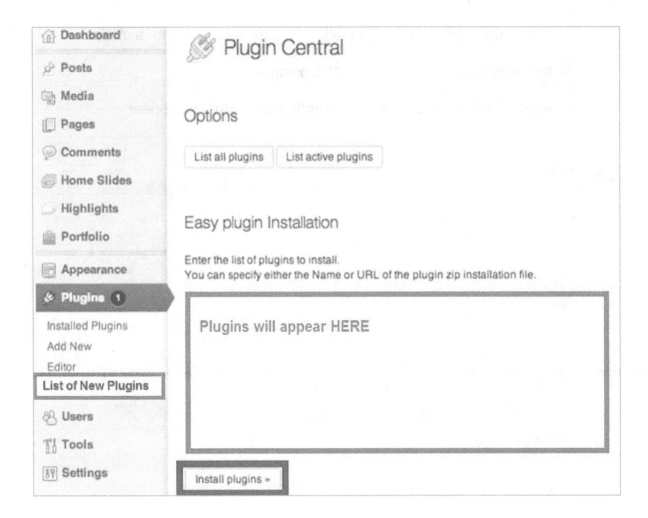

All of the plugins mentioned in the previous section can easily be found through the WordPress' search query and installed as above.

Manually Installing the Plugins

In case you have downloaded a plugin that is not available in the database you can install it manually as well.

To install the plugin through the WordPress dashboard:

1. Download the plugin you want to install;

2. Unzip the file to an easily accessible location on your desktop;

3. From your dashboard, Go to **"Plugins"** and **"Add New"**;

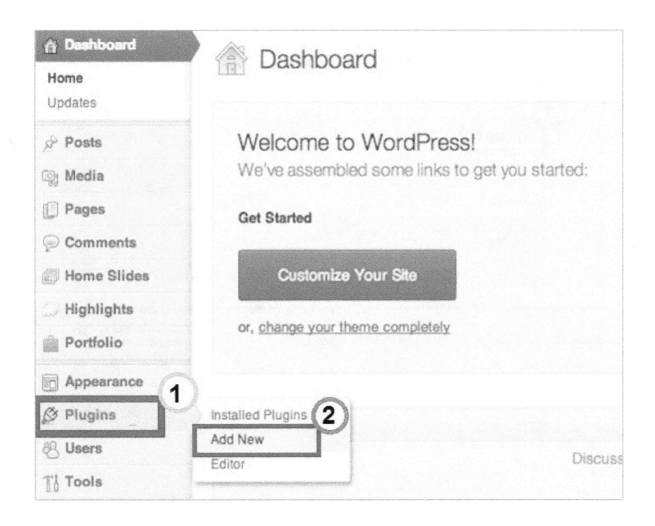

4. Click, "**Upload**" and then "**Browse**" (see picture below);

5. Locate the unzipped folder for the plugin and click open;

6. Click "**Install Now**";

The new plugin will automatically be uploaded to your blog and activated.

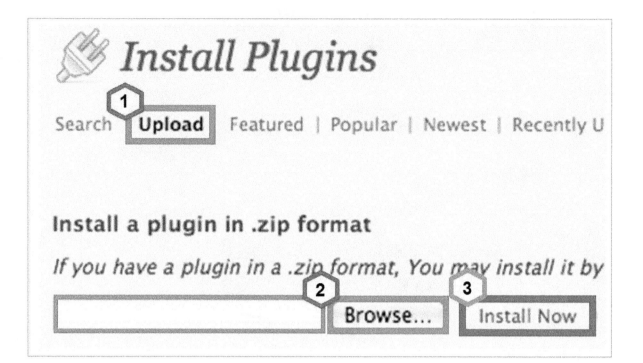

Step#4: Upload Some Content

WordPress likes to add certain welcoming posts on every new website. Hence our first task will be to delete these posts before adding new content. But before that, we must understand the types of content.

The Types of Content

There are primarily two types of content that you will be interacting with on your website. These are the posts and pages.

Pages

A page is a more permanent type of content. It structures how visitors can navigate through your website. Primary examples include the About page and Contact page. A page contains content that ought to be made readily available for all the visitors through menus.

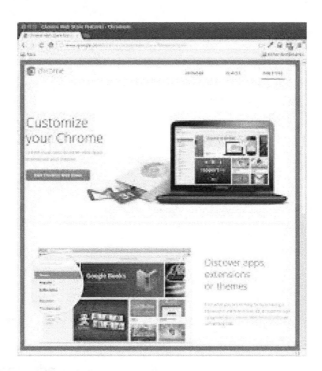

Posts

A post is simply an article that engages a reader with information on different topics. This content can easily be added/removed at will without harming the efficiency of your website. Hence, posts form the bulk on the structure/architecture of your website and can easily be categorized through the use of tags and categories.

We will start by first removing the default content that WordPress likes to add to any new website, followed by adding new posts and then finally creating pages and organizing our content.

Deleting Default Content

1. Login in to WordPress Admin panel.

2. In the left hand side bar, click **Posts>All Posts**;

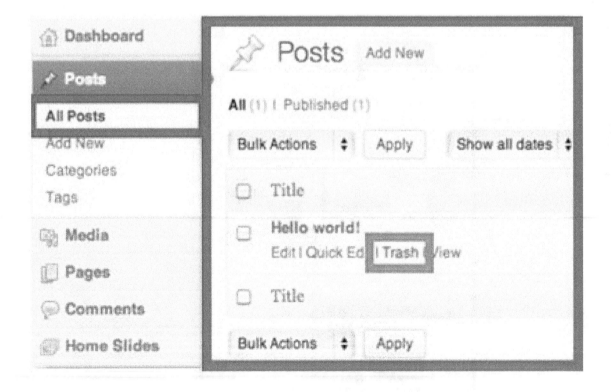

3. Delete the post titled "Hello World" by clicking "**Trash**" underneath it.

4. Next go to **Pages** > **All Pages**.

5. Delete "**Sample Page**" by clicking "**Trash**"

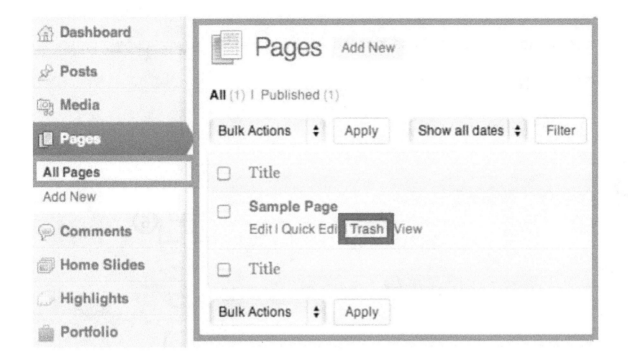

Adding New Content

Adding Posts

1. Log in to your WordPress dashboard by going to: www.your-worpress-site.com/wp-admin.

2. Go to, **"Posts"** > **"Add New"**

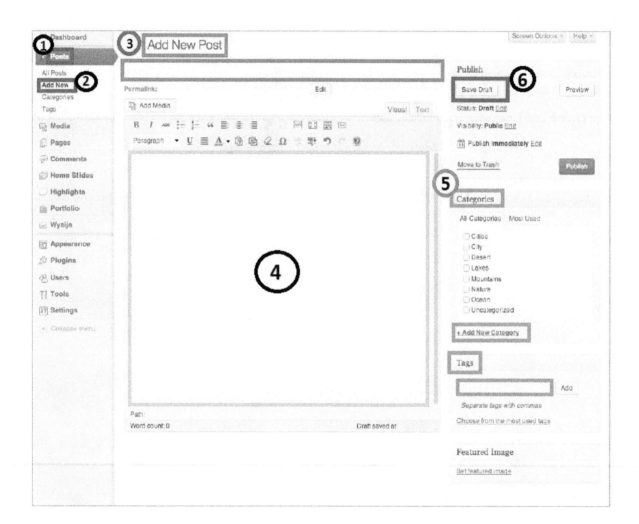

3. Enter a title for your post;

4. Type/paste your post in the body section;

5. Categorize your post by selecting or adding relevant category and tags from the right hand side.

6. Save it as a draft by clicking the "Save Draft" button

It is a good practice to save draft using "Save Draft" button until you are ready to publish your post. Make the post more engaging by featuring images:

7. Select "Set Featured Image" button on the right hand sidebar.

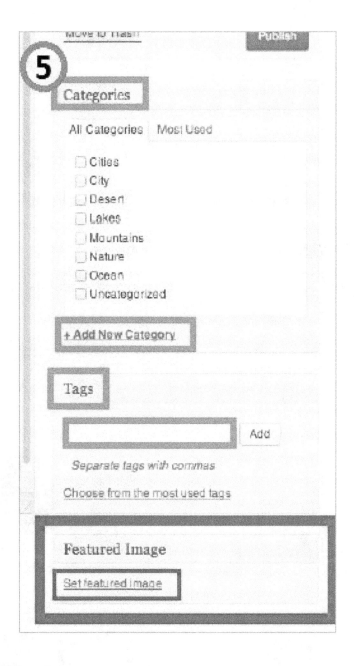

8. From the dialog box:

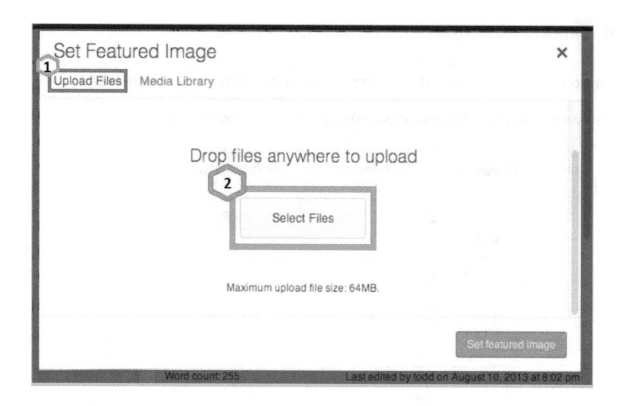

9. Click "**Upload Files**" link located in the upper, left-hand corner of the screen.

10. Click "**Select Files**" and locate the image you intend to feature on your post.

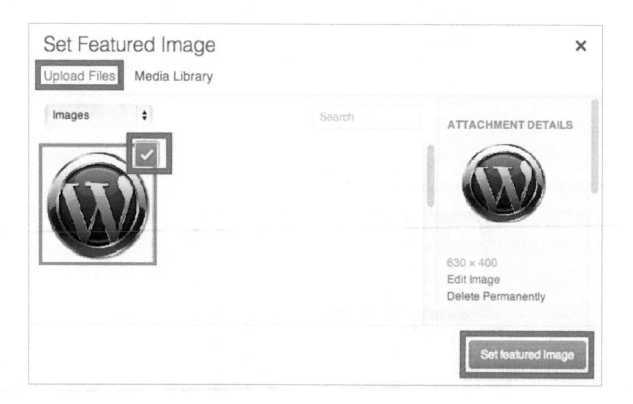

11. Click "**Set Featured Image**". The image will show up in your "Edit Post" window.

Publish the post. It will automatically appear on your Blog page.

Adding Pages

In this section we will be adding four prominent pages to your website:

1. Home Page

2. Blog Page

3. About Page

4. Contact Page

Later we will customize each page individually so you can firmly grasp the process.

HOME PAGE

This is the first page visitors land on and hence one of the most visited page on your website.

1. Log in to your WordPress dashboard;

2. Select "**Pages**" > "**Add New**" from the left-hand side bar;

3. Add "**Home**" as the title of the page.

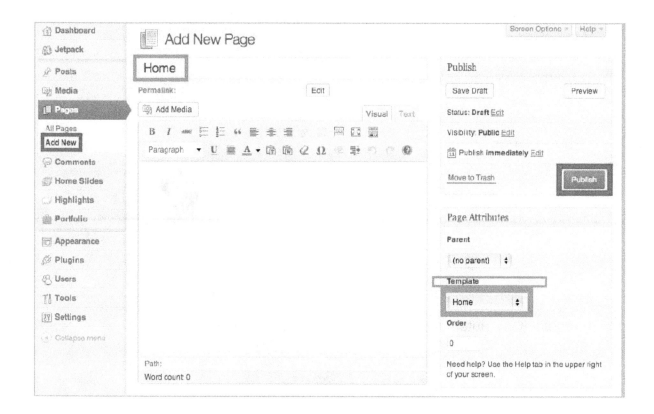

4. Select the "**Home**" template from the drop down menu.

5. Select "**Publish**".

A page titled "**Home**" will be added to your website.

BLOG PAGE

Create this page exactly as you created the Home page — change the title to Blog.

We will tweak it up later.

This page lists excerpts or interesting snippets from your most recent blog posts. Each snippet should contain a Featured Image and a few lines of text to engage the reader. We will configure your posts soon enough!

But first, let's create the remaining pages.

ABOUT PAGE

This is the page where you introduce yourself, your blog, your services or your business. An about page may contain an image.

1. Select "**Pages**" > "**Add New**";

2. Add "**About**" as the title of the page;

3. Select "**Visual**" tab;

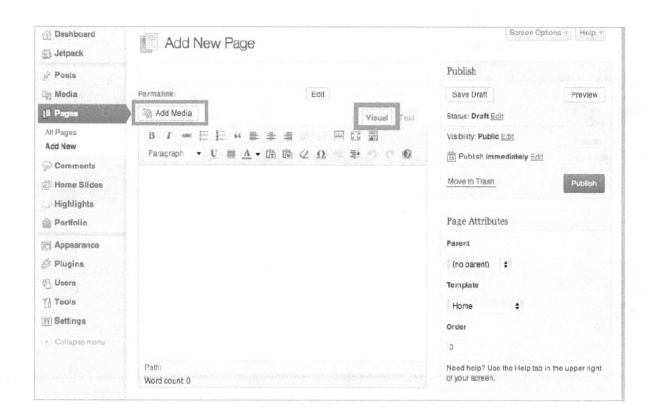

4. Click "**Add Media**";

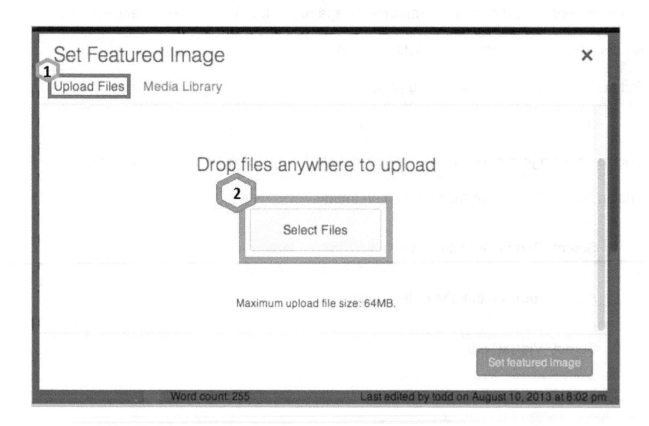

5. Insert image by selecting "**Upload**" followed by selecting the image.

6. Set the thumbnail size to **150x150**

7. Click "Insert Into Page".

8. Click "**Publish**".

CONTACT PAGE

This is the page from where visitors can get in touch with you. We will be using a Fast Secure Contact Form (FSCF) that will aid you in preventing automated spam.

1. Select "**Pages**" > "**Add New**";

2. Add "**Contact**" as the title;

3. Select "**Visual**" tab;

4. Add the FSCF code [si-contact-form form='1'] in the text field where you would add normal text;

5. Click "**Publish**".

This will add a contact form on your Contact page. It will automatically forward any requests/queries to the email address you had added when you installed WordPress. To change your email address:

1. Go to, "**Plugins**" > "**FS Contact Form Options**";

2. Change the address in "**E-mail**" and "**E-mail Confirmation**" sections;

3. Click "**Update Options**" to finish.

Now it's time to make all these pages more user-friendly and engaging.

Importing Content

In case you already have a blog on another platform and you want to transfer certain content to your newly created website on WordPress, then it is wise to import the files instead of uploading them individually.

1. Visit your dashboard;

2. Go to, "**Tools**" > "**Import**";

3. Select "**WordPress**";

4. Click on the, **"Choose File"** button and navigate to where you have stored your content from the previous blog. This will be an XML file.

An XML file is automatically generated as you export all your content from your previous blog (mostly for the sake of backup). The file is easily recognized and extracted by WordPress and most of your formatting will remain the same;

5. Click, **"Upload file and import"**;

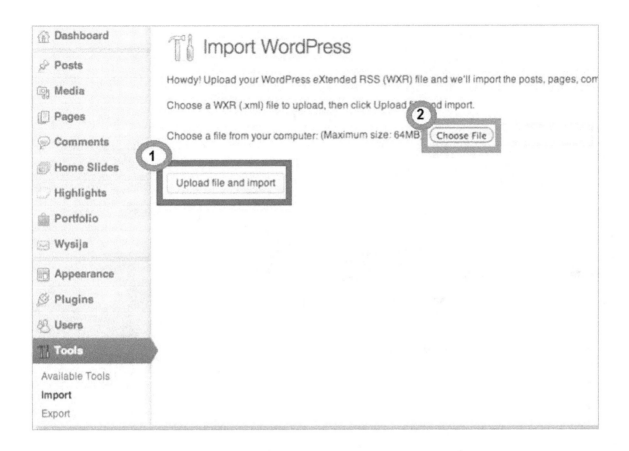

6. You will be prompted to select your username from the drop down menu for "**Import Author**";

7. Make sure to check, "**Download and import file attachments**";

8. Finally, click "**Submit**";

9. After all of the data is imported, you'll see a message stating, "**All done. Have fun!**"

Further Customizing Your Pages

The Home Page

Your home page can have three different sections where you can add content. These include:

1. **Home Slides** – They appear right below the navigation bar and *can* display titles and short descriptions of your selected content.

2. **Highlights** – These appear underneath the slides and are normally used to explain what your business/website is about.

3. **Blog Posts** – This is an automatically generated section displaying your recent posts.

Let's start with adding slides to your homepage.

Adding Slides to the Home Page

This is similar to adding a post or a page except that it is devoid of any body-text. That space is replaced by a featured image. To add the slides:

1. Log in to your dashboard;

2. Go to "**Home Slides**" > "**Add New**";

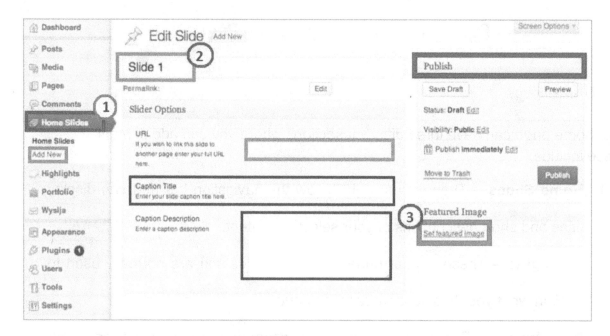

3. Add a title like "**Slide 1**"— the title won't get displayed;

4. Click "**Set Featured Image**",

5. Next, click "**Upload Files**" and finally "**Select Files**";

6. Navigate to the pictures you wish to add to the slides.

7. Finally, click "**Set Featured Image**".

8. If you want the slide to link to another page on your website or another webpage, **enter the URL**;

9. Enter a Caption and its description (Optional);

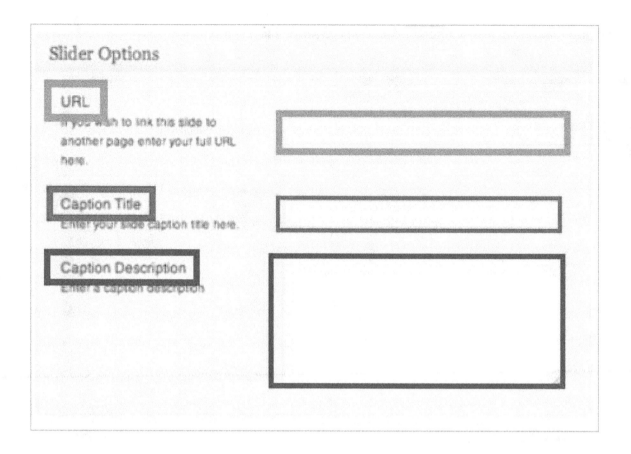

10. Save your Draft until you're ready to publish.

11. Publish the Slide when you want it to show up on your Home page.

12. Repeat the steps above to create more slides for your home page.

Now it's time to add highlights

Adding Highlights to the Home Page

1. Login/visit your dashboard;

2. Go to "**Highlights**" > "**Add New**";

3. Add a title — *it will get displayed.* It will be visible on top of your highlight;

4. Add some content. Make it short and to the point—it's a highlight!

5. Add a URL if you want your Highlight to link to another page;

6. Choose an icon you want to use for the highlight;

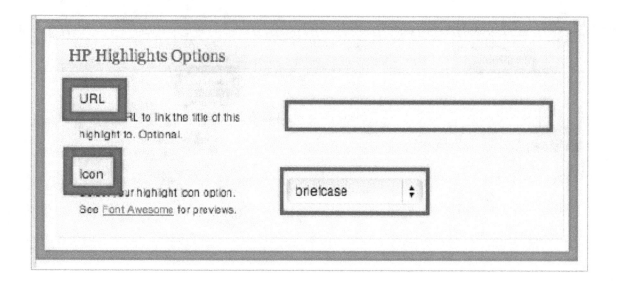

7. Save it as a draft as long as you're not ready to publish it;

8. Publish your Highlight. It will show up on your Home page;

9. Repeat Steps 2-8 and create more highlights.

Turning Comments OFF for Pages

It is advisable to restrict comments to your blog posts and turn them off for all the other pages.

1. Log in to your dashboard.

2. Go to "**Pages**" > "**All Pages**" in the left-hand menu;

3. Click "**Screen Options**" in the upper, right-hand corner;

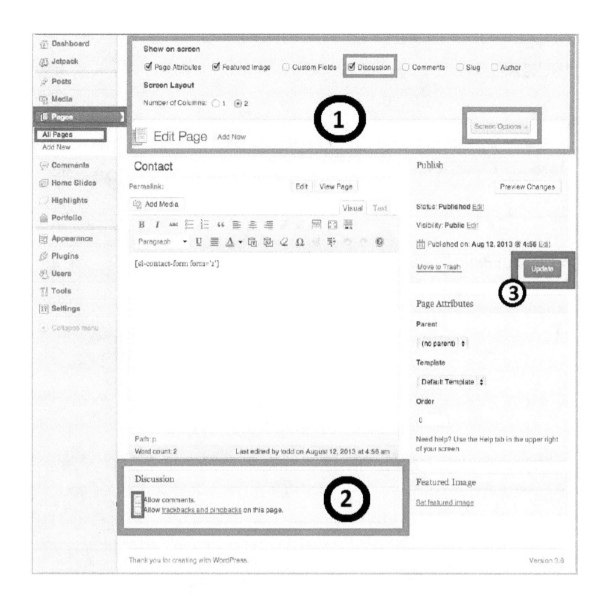

4. Select "**Discussion**";

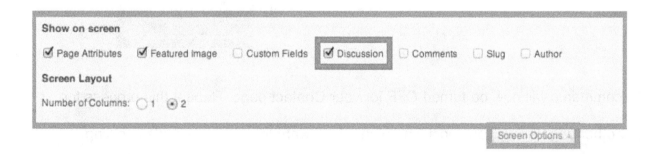

5. Uncheck both, "**Allow Comments**" and "**Allow trackbacks and pingbacks on this page**";

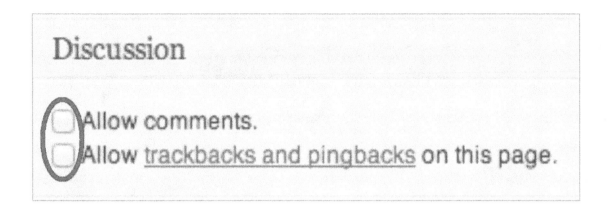

6. Click the "**Update**".

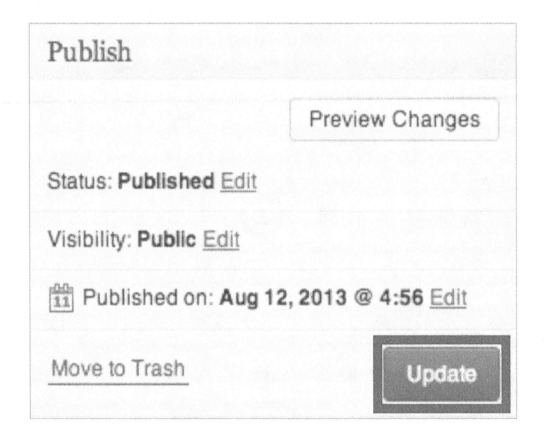

All comments will now be turned OFF for your Contact page. Repeat this process for any other page as well any post where you don't want to have comments showing.

Step#5: Configure – WordPress, Theme, Plugins

Configuring WordPress

There are three configurations that need to be made. These include:

1. Creating and setting the main menu;

2. Setting the Pages –Home page and the Blog page;

3. Restructuring the URLs.

These configurations are not tedious and only require some mouse work on your behalf.

Creating and Setting the Main Menu

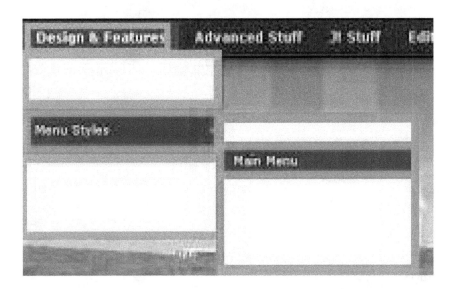

The main menu is essential to properly displaying the navigation menus to all the visitors to your website. Setting this menu ensures that every page on your website will display a standard navigation menu to the visitors. In order to set the main menu for your website:

1. Log in to your WordPress dashboard at:

   www.your-worpress-site.com/wp-admin

2. Navigate to, "**Appearance**" > "**Menus**" in the left-hand column.

3. In the, "**Menu Name**" box, type "Main Menu". This is the heading that **will** appear on the website you would have finally created. Think of these as road signs that direct the driver to the right destinations. If these are not carfully created, you can easily jeopardize the whole navigation for the visitor. The rule of thumb is to make them short, to the point and in an easy to understand language.

4. Create your menu by clicking "**Create Menu**;

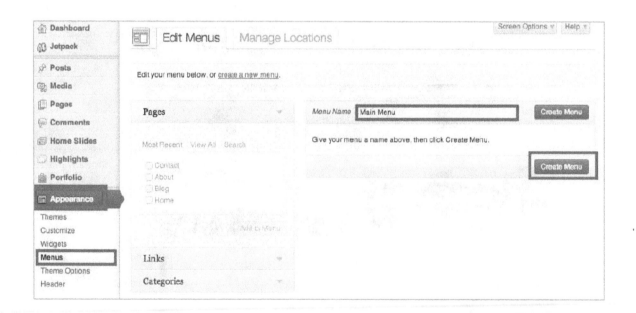

5. From the page:

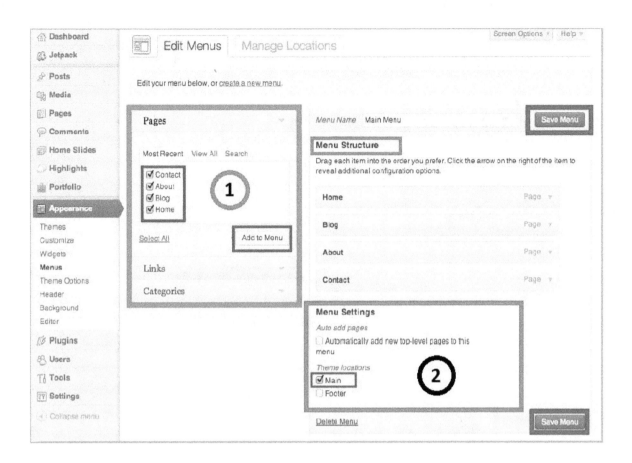

6. As you can see, the page is divided into several sections.

    a. The pages that you have created so far

    b. The structure of the menu i.e. how will it get displayed to the visitor

    c. The settings for the main menu i.e. how you would have it appear (in the side bar, or in the footer etc. We'll deal with this at length later)

7. Select all four pages that you created earlier: Home, Blog, Contact, and About.

8. Now select "**Add to Menu**" to add the pages to the menu you have created.

9. Notice that all pages that you created earlier (Home, Contact, Blog, About) show up in the menu. To order them, simply drag and drop them with your mouse.

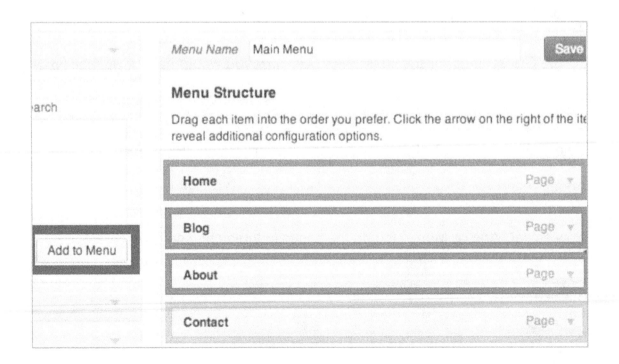

10. Make sure the box for "**Main**" is checked.

11. Save this configuration by clicking, "**Save Menu**".

This completes all of the steps for adding a menu to your website. You should now have all of the pages showing up in the navigation menu of your site.

Set the Home Page and Blog Page

The aim of this setting is to ensure that all of your important blog post excerpts, slides, and highlight are displayed on the Home page of your website. Furthermore, WordPress will show all the blog post excerpts on your Blog page as well.

1. Log in to your WordPress dashboard at:

   www.your-worpress-site.com/wp-admin

2. Go to, "**Setting**" > "**Reading**" from the left-hand column;

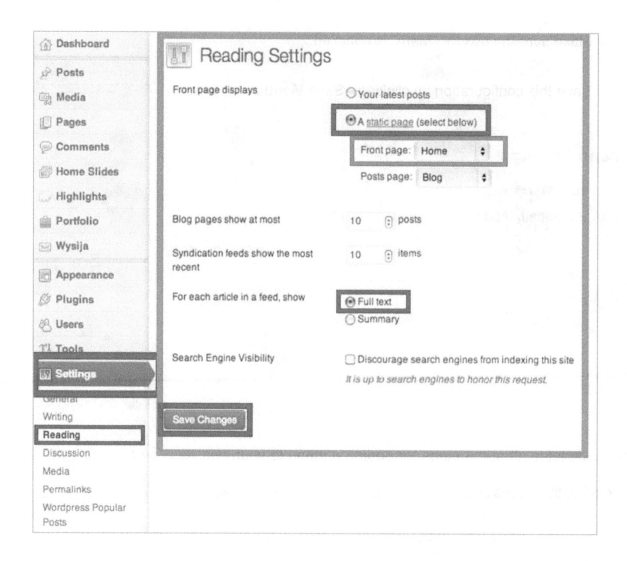

3. From the Reading Settings on the right hand side, select "**A Static Page**" from "**Front page displays**" options;

For "**Front Page**" select, "**Home**" from the drop down menu;

4. Select "Blog" for the "Posts page".

5. Set the number of blog pages you want to display on your Blog page on, "Blog pages show at most"

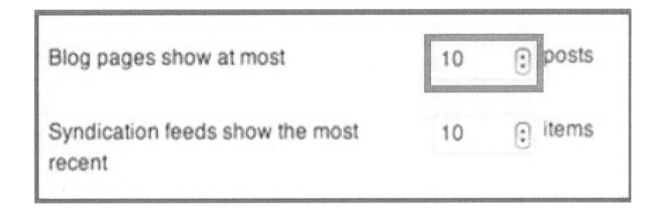

6. Click "Save Changes" to complete the configuration.

Changing the Structure of Your URLs

Basically you will be restructuring how your "Permalinks" will display your post titles as a URL, so instead of displaying www.your-worpress-site.com/p=?123post they will get displayed as www.your-worpress-site.com/my-latest-post, which is a lot easier for people and search engines to find.

Restructuring the URLs allows visitors to easily remember your link and secondly they improve your website's search engine ranking (as you can add the target keyword into the title!)

Here's how you can accomplish both of those things in four easy steps.

1. Log in to your dashboard;

2. In the left-hand menu, go to, "**Settings**" > "**Permalinks**";

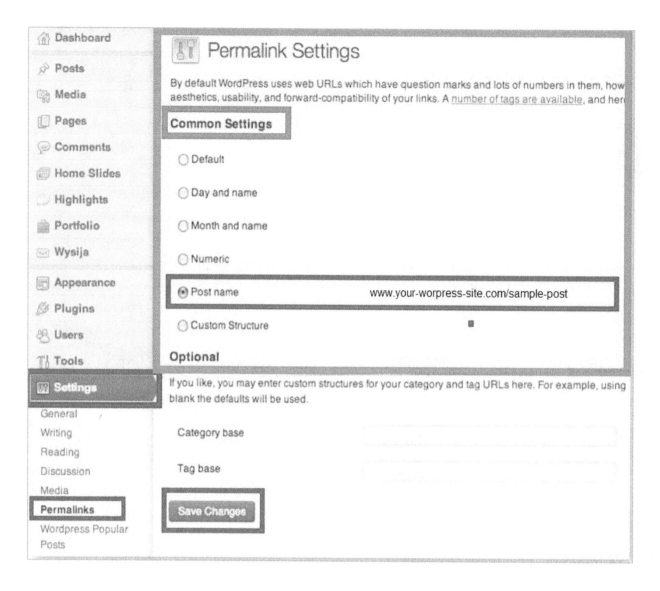

3. Select, "**Post Name**" under the "**Common Settings**" section.

4. Click on the, "Save Changes" button at the bottom to save your settings.

And that completes our configuration of WordPress. We only had to make three simple changes, and now we're ready to go and configure our plugins.

So let's keep moving.

Configure Your Theme

Every theme you download can be reconfigured to meet your demands. The WordPress dashboard allows you a wide range of configurations for your theme.

General

These options affect the overall state of your website. Let's go over what each one of them will do.

The general tab is available in the Appearance section of your Dashboard. To get to the "General" options tab, do the following:

1. Log in to your dashboard;

2. Go to, "**Appearance**" > "**Theme Options**";

3. Click on the "**General**" tab on the left.

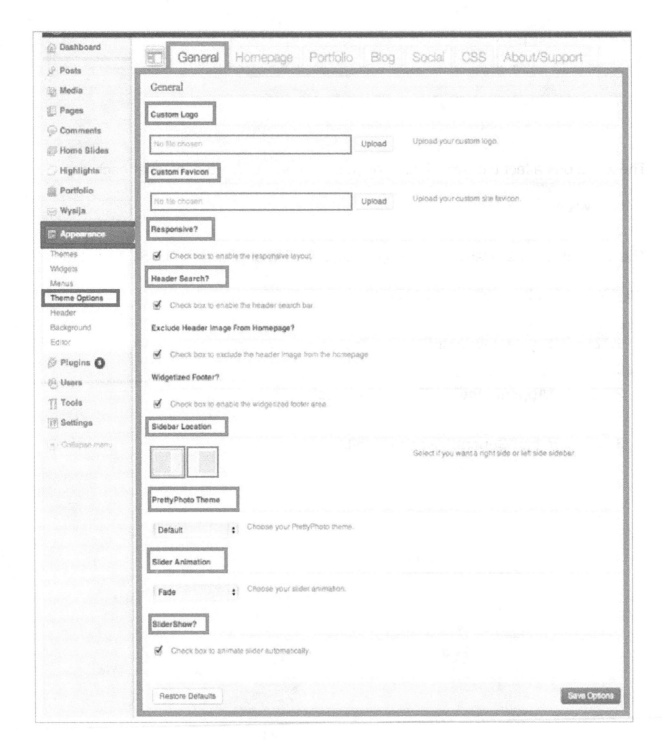

You'll see a plethora of customizable options to your right. Lets see what each of them does for you. The following options are available:

1. **Custom Logo** —if you have designed a logo for your brand, then this is the place from where it can be uploaded. A logo goes a long way with a homepage tagline and will be discussed in the next section.

2. **Custom Favicon** – This is the tiny icon you can normally see atop the tab of any browser when you visit different websites. In case you don't, then it means that the webmaster for that website has not created one. We won't upload one just now.

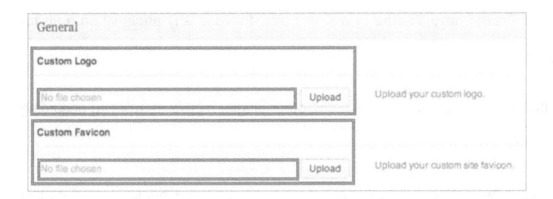

3. **Responsive** — as you know, a responsive website is one that can easily adjust to the size of the browser it's being displayed on. Keep this option checked to make your website mobile device friendly.

4. **Header Search** — selecting this adds a search bar in the header of your theme.

5. **Exclude Header Image from Homepage** — Keep this checked. Consider it as a search engine tweak to make your webpage blip as "legit" on the search engine's radars;

6. **Widgetized Footer** — with this checked, you can easily add widgets at the footer of your web page. We will add some widgets in a while.

7. **Sidebar Location** — you have the option of aligning the sidebar either to your webpage's right or to its left. It is customary to add it to your right.

A lot of themes come pre-equipped with certain plugins and the option to configure that plugin will be found here. In this case we have used the free Pytheas responsive theme and **PrettyPhoto Theme** is a plugin that enlarges any photo when a visitor clicks on it.

If your theme comes equipped with some other plugin, modify its working according to your liking.

8. **Slider Animation** — if you have added slides to your home page, then this option will allow you to control how the slider on your home page transitions from one slide to the next. Choose any option that suits your liking.

9. **Slider Show** — this options lets you toggle between an automatic slider and a manual one. If it is checked, then the slider will automatically change from slide to slide. If unchecked, the visitor will have to use the slider to go to the next slide. Keep it checked, if the visitor likes a slide, s/he can always slide the slider back/forward.

10. **Save Options** — once you have finished configuring your general tab, select this option to save all the changes.

11. **Reset Defaults** — this will reset all the changes you have made to the theme at hand and restore WordPress' default settings.

The Homepage

The following changes will affect the features and content of your Home page. As the title might imply, all of the settings that you change on the Homepage tab will affect the content and features on your Home page.

Almost all of them are self explanatory; we'll discuss them in enough details so that you know what they can do for you. To access your homepage theme configuration panel:

1. Login/visit your dashboard;

2. Go to, "**Appearance**" > "**Theme Options**";

3. Click on the "**Homepage**" tab on the left;

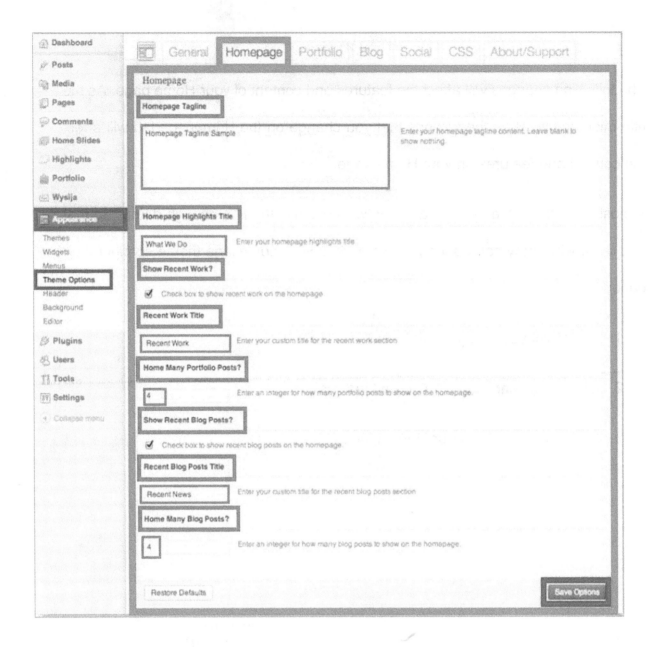

Now let's talk about all the options you can change there:

4. **Homepage Tagline** — let's your write your own Homepage Tagline. NOTE: this will not appear under the slides or the highlights but rather on top of the explorer's bar;

5. **Homepage Highlights Title** — you have already designed your highlights, now you can tweak that experience for the visitor by adding a title that shows up right above the row of Highlights on the Home page. E.g. if your highlights

are showing what you or your company is doing, you can simply write "What We Do" in the text field provided.

6. **Show Recent Work** — this option is linked to your portfolio (which we will configure in the next section!). In summary, your recent work is added to your latest Portfolio and if you have this box checked that recent Portfolio piece will show up on the Home page. Select this option.

7. **Recent Work Title** — this once again is related to your portfolio. Any text you ad over here will appear as the title that goes right above your row of Portfolio pieces;

8. **How Many Portfolio Posts** — specify the number of Portfolio posts you want to display;

9. **Show Recent Blog Posts** — select this option as it will display your latest blog articles for the show;

10. **Recent Blog Posts Title** — this allows you to change the title that's displayed above the **Recent Blog Posts** section;

11. **How Many Blog Posts** — configure the number of posts that get displayed at once;

12. **Save Options** — do not forget to save the changes you have made so far! Even selecting another tab may revert the changes;

13. **Reset Defaults** — erases all progress and takes you back to the age of WordPress default settings for Home page, where you began from.

Your Portfolio

1. From your dashboard, go to "**Appearance**" > "**Theme Options**";

2. Click on the "Portfolio" tab in the middle;

3. **Portfolio Posts per Page** — this sets the number of portfolio posts to show if you decide to use a "Portfolio" template for your webpage. It's a bit advanced and for now leaving it blank will neither harm the interactivity of your webpage nor the user-experience.

4. **Save Options** - Make sure to save any changes you make to the "Portfolio" tab before moving on to another tab.

Blog

The options available in this tab allow you to change the features associated with individual blog posts. To start configuring your blog page:

1. From your dashboard go to "**Appearance**" > "**Theme Options**";

2. Select the "**Blog**" tab ;

After you get there, you'll find the following four options. You need to select all of them:

1. Featured Images On Single Posts —

You can set a featured image for each blog post when you publish it. This featured image will always appear besides the excerpt from the post on you "Blog" page as well as appear at the top of the single blog post. By turning it ON, you increase the chances of a visitor clicking through to your blog post. This is primarily because images are easier to locate then reading through each excerpt, hence the tip: select the featured image wisely. Make your featured image speak as much about the post as possible.

2. Author Bio —

This is the short biography of the author of the blog post (sometimes you can even have guest bloggers, hence even more useful for such times).

3. **Tags** —

Tags make it easier to categorize your posts. This aids not only in aiding the visitor search for relevant posts or when you are organizing your content, but also for search engines to rank your posts high on its search engine results page. Tags are a way of labeling and organizing posts with a label. Checking this shows these tags at the end of each post.

4. **Related Posts** —

Your blog posts are a great way of increasing the traffic to your website *from* your posts. If all your posts are tagged properly, then WordPress can show other posts with similar tags as **Related Posts** to the visitor. By checking this box you will let WordPress show thumbnails and titles of other posts in the same category at the bottom of each single blog post.

5. **Save Options** — as always, save the changes before turning your attention to the next heading or tab!

6. **Reset Defaults** — the button that makes you wonder "they could have added an undo button!"

Social

We also need to add your social icons so that your visitors can click on them. Though we have already added some cool social plugins for you to install you're your website, you should still know how to interact with your website design from your dashboard. These social icons will be located in the menu to the right and will be visible on every page.

To get to the "Social" options tab:

1. Visit your WordPress Dashboard;

2. Go to, **"Appearance"** > **"Theme Options"**;

3. Click on the "**Social**" tab in the middle.

Here's what you should do:

1. **Social** — select this checkbox to show/hide the social icons in the menu bar.

2. **Add your URLs** — for each of the social networks listed and for which you have a profile (in case you don't make them!), follow the following format:

   a) http://www.facebook.com/yourworpresssite (can be anything that visitors can relate to your original website

   b) http://www.twitter.com/YWPsite (shortened)

3. **Save Options** — we hope you're getting used to the idea of saving your work in progress! Still, make sure to save any changes you have made to the "Social" tab before moving on to another tab;

4. **Reset Defaults** — Reset it and your visitors will be dangling in digital space trying to find your social profiles before finally finding their way AWAY from them.

About/Support

The "About/Support" tab provides links and information about the developer of the theme that you have used on your website.

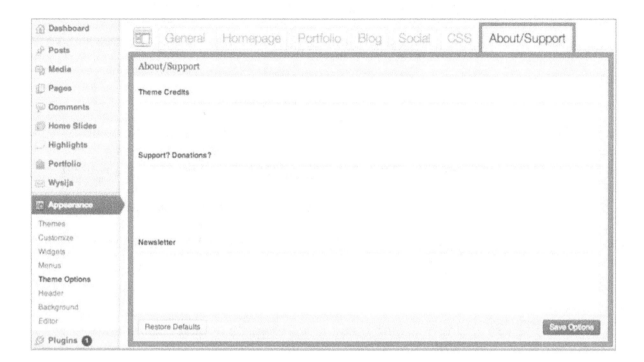

And with that last tab, we're finished configuring all of the options available for the theme that you may select for your website.

Final Words

From the very beginning, our goal had been to prepare a guide to WordPress that will bring this great and powerful website platform within the reach of layman. Throughout this guide we have tried our level best to walk you through the process of creating your website.

To recap, we began by understanding the basic elements of a website, followed by creating and registering a domain name and hosting it on a server. Next we walked you through the steps through which we installed the WordPress platform, its responsive themes, and plugins that optimized your website for both the visitors and the search engines.

Once, the website's structure was ready we moved towards adding relevant content to the website. This included creating and configuring pages and posts. Finally, we configured all the aspects of the website so that it is ready to be left over to the search engines and the visitors.

We hope that by the time you'll reach this chapter, you will already have created a website using WordPress. We believe that this website will be optimized not only for search engines but is also capable of providing a great user-experience.

Wishing you all the best for your future digital endeavors!